My Journey

My childhood was not a great one, but I've come to realize that life is easier when I replace the chip on my shoulder, anger in my heart, and bitterness in my mind with peace from within. So many of us can't say that, which is sad. We must share the tragedies of our childhood and teach what we have learned to help others.

I now believe that everything I went through was essential in making me the amazing person I am today. I've endured this challenging journey so I can be wise and help others who also have endured this kind of pain. It is my soul's journey, as I am just a vessel for my soul.

It's been a rough life, but I have no regrets, for I love who I am today. I'm also sure I have more lessons to learn, but now I can see and understand why these lessons are coming to me. You know how we all say, "If I knew then what I know now . . ." So true. But some lessons keep coming to us until we finally listen and get it.

Now I accept everything that comes my way, and I let the universe guide me, for my spirit knows where I belong. Join me on this journey.

Acknowledgments

Thanks to:

Elaine Minty, for helping with my book.

Linda McQuoid—I couldn't get to where I am today without your help.

Patrick Flaherty, for taking beautiful photos.

Hay Publishing, for allowing this dream to come true.

God has a perfect plan for us.
He never does it all at once.
Just step by step
Because he wants to teach us
To walk by faith, not by sight.
—Author unknown

Preface

This is a book about my journey to find my life's purpose and achieve inner peace. After years of wondering *why me*, I have had to take another look and change *why me* to *I was meant to learn and help others*.

I wrote this book to help anyone who has been abused, so that you too can get past the pain and find inner peace—and most importantly, know that you are not alone.

I hope my story can help people see that their journey is worth it—that *they* are worth it. To see the good in what they learned instead of seeing only the pain.

We all can overcome difficult times in our lives and find that inner peace we so desire. I hope the amazing people who read about my journey can see the positive in their lives now, in their twenties and thirties, and not have to wait until their forties like I did.

Table of Contents

In Memory of My Best Friend

My longest relationship ever with a male was with my dog of twelve years. He had to be euthanized because of an illness. I took this very hard. The only constant thing in my life, he always said good-bye and then greeted me at the door when I returned. His love was unconditional. He had no idea he was a little guy. He thought he was big and captured many hearts.

You will forever be missed, Harley.
July 12, 2000-December 31, 2012

I dedicate this book to my family

To my mother—I finally understand your journey, which also has not always been easy, and I know you love me.

To my amazing niece, for having such innocence and showing me such true love.

To my children, my angels, for picking me as their mother. You are the reason I found such strength to live and love life, by watching how you live your lives, and for that I will be forever grateful.

Balboa Press books may be ordered through booksellers or by contacting:

Balboa Press
A Division of Hay House
1663 Liberty Drive
Bloomington, IN 47403
www.balboapress.com
1-(877) 407-4847

Because of the dynamic nature of the Internet, any web addresses or links contained in
this book may have changed since publication and may no longer be valid. The views
expressed in this work are solely those of the author and do not necessarily reflect the
views of the publisher, and the publisher hereby disclaims any responsibility for them.

The author of this book does not dispense medical advice or prescribe the use
of any technique as a form of treatment for physical, emotional, or medical
problems without the advice of a physician, either directly or indirectly. The
intent of the author is only to offer information of a general nature to help you
in your quest for emotional and spiritual well-being. In the event you use any
of the information in this book for yourself, which is your constitutional right,
the author and the publisher assume no responsibility for your actions.

Any people depicted in stock imagery provided by Thinkstock are models,
and such images are being used for illustrative purposes only.
Certain stock imagery © Thinkstock.

ISBN: 978-1-4525-7098-3 (sc)
ISBN: 978-1-4525-7100-3 (hc)
ISBN: 978-1-4525-7099-0 (e)

Library of Congress Control Number: 2013905272

Printed in the United States of America.

Balboa Press rev. date: 3/22/2013

My Innocence Lost

DAISY ANN RHODES

BALBOA.
PRESS
A DIVISION OF HAY HOUSE

This Is My Story

Not many of us remember our earliest days, and I am thankful for that. There's a reason our brain protects us sometimes from certain events. My earliest memory of any part of my life is from when I was about four years of age. It's a memory of my birthfather. He did things no father should ever do to his daughter, or any child. This man sexually molested me for years.

My mother was only fifteen years old when she became pregnant with me. In 1967, that was a major sin. My grandmother did not want my mother to have the baby. Mom had a choice: a coat-hanger abortion or a wedding. She decided to get married, with no idea that the road she had chosen would bring such despair.

She was sixteen and he was twenty-two when they were married. Unable to wear white because she was expecting, my mother wore blue.

From what I recall of my childhood, my birthfather was abusive to my mother. I remember the beatings. I remember being left alone a lot with my father, as my mother worked a lot. She had to pay the bills. It was her money that kept food on the table. She had no choice.

My mother was so young when she had me that we never had that bonding experience mothers and babies should have.

How could a baby love a baby? She had no idea what I needed. I was deprived of the bond that every child needs so much. This explains my need for such affection today.

She suspected I was being abused, and she says she asked me about it when I was five years old. Well, of course I said no. He told me to say no or my mother would take me away. What little girl wants to lose her daddy? I mean, it wasn't all bad. He took me shopping, to Ontario Place. We had fun when my mother was working. Every little girl wants her mother and father. I was too young to understand my fear and confusion.

When my mother decided it was time for her to leave, my birthfather wouldn't let her take me. So she left me behind for what seemed to me to be days, but it was only hours. She called the police, and I remember being in the police car. They asked me if my dad touched me. I remember urinating in my pants because I was so scared, so I said no. How intimidating it was, being in a police car. That is no way to ask a child about such a sensitive subject; neither, for that matter, is a counselor's office. The questioning needs to be done in a natural setting, with someone who can offer trust and patience. Just picture any little child looking up to authority. This is why so many will not talk. Very intimidating.

I fall, I rise,

I make mistakes.

I live, I learn,

I've been hurt.

But I'm alive.

I'm human and I'm not perfect,

But I'm thankful.

—Author unknown

I don't remember how, but somehow my mother got custody of me, and we moved into my grandmother's house. But the abuse continued, since my birthfather still had visitation rights. In the '70s, they didn't protect children the way they do now. Since I denied the abuse, it looked as though my mother was making up stories.

My grandmother didn't care for me. She blamed me for ruining her daughter's life, and it made her angry. She wasn't a pleasant woman. To her, I was just a mistake, and she took her bitterness and disappointment out on the only person she could: me.

When it finally came to blows, I can't remember exactly what she said, but I remember yelling and screaming at her, "You hate me! It's not my fault! I never asked to be born. I don't want to live, I don't want to be here, and I didn't ask to live." It finally came pouring out. I was so angry and hurt. I asked God to take me every Sunday when I was at Sunday school. No child should feel like this.

After that, it was like something came over my grandmother. From that moment on, she cared. I no longer felt that she hated me. She hugged me, and I felt loved. Her tone, her attitude— everything changed. I can only assume she realized I really was innocent of everything. This had not been my choice.

During this time that we lived with my grandmother, my mom continued to work a lot, so I spent time with a babysitter who lived across the road. This babysitter had sons my age and older. When I was home from kindergarten, she would send me to play in the basement while she made supper upstairs. One of her older sons would always come down too. At first he would play with me, but then things started to change, and he slowly started molesting me.

This is just the way life is, I thought. It's all I knew. It felt so wrong, and they always said "Keep it a secret," which was confusing. But a child doesn't need to understand these things to adapt to them. We learn to live outside our body. We are not there when it's happening. We take ourselves somewhere else.

Years later, when Grandma was near the end of her days, she had bad diabetes and her kidneys were failing, so she had to move to a nursing home. It became an amazing time to really get to know her. When she was there, she needed to be bathed, and she did not want the nurses to help—yet she couldn't do it on her own, so I volunteered.

Grandma was so embarrassed being naked in front of her granddaughter and vulnerable while I bathed her. For some reason, I am very aware of others' feelings, and I knew how she felt. She deserved to have her dignity, so one day I also stripped down. I told her, "Grandma, we are in this together." After the shock wore off, she laughed. She then looked forward to our time together.

Sometimes in our lives, we need to put ourselves in the other person's shoes. We should always be aware of and try to understand how the other person we are dealing with may feel. Some of us have this ability to be aware of others and our surroundings, and some just don't understand.

I learned so much from my grandmother at this time. Wow, what a family history lesson. We really should take the time to know our grandparents. They have lived such amazing lives. Those people sitting on a bench, driving slowly, walking slowly—they have lived and have seen things that we can't even imagine.

Near the last few months of her life, Grandma really came out of her shell. This grumpy lady told dirty jokes, flirted with the old guys, and got drunk off the rum raisin pudding. I had never seen her laugh like that, ever. I am so glad we had that time together.

I don't think my mother had ever had so much fun with her own mother before either. Our family had a lot of deep-down belly laughs during this time. It's a time we will never forget.

My grandmother passed away on Valentine's Day, 2006. How fitting—her husband had passed away when she was thirty-three, and she'd always remained true to her vows. She was now with her husband, who I know greeted her and they did a waltz.

I can honestly say I would not remain single if I lost my husband at an early age. How amazing and respectful this lady was.

I miss and love you dearly, Grandma. I know you are my guardian angel.

My Childhood

I remember things happening in an apple orchard. Even to this day, I feel sick when I'm near an orchard. Again, thank God for those mental blocks that keep the frightening details from coming back. The abuse continued until the age of eight or nine. I was too afraid to speak up, but I know there were other little girls being harmed. I had to stop bringing friends over because I was so afraid of what he would do to them. My mother had told me the neighbors' mom had contacted her to talk about my father. I'm unaware of what happened, but he moved shortly after.

My mother finally moved me to a town two hours away, which stopped the abuse. I wonder what it's really like to have the innocence of a child and not a care in the world.

My father still had visits with me, but now he had a girlfriend, so the abuse for me was over. We went camping with his girlfriend, and we did fun things when we had time together. But the fear and the memories were always there. They don't go away, but you push them aside. It's called survival mode.

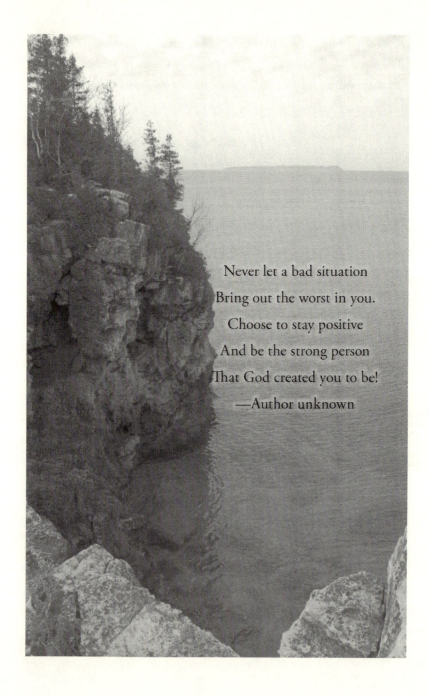

Never let a bad situation
Bring out the worst in you.
Choose to stay positive
And be the strong person
That God created you to be!
—Author unknown

My mother once said she wished she had given me up for adoption. I was heartbroken for years to think she never wanted me. This is, however, not what she meant. She meant that if she had given me up, I would have had a different life, and she could have saved me from abuse.

But who knows? We can only assume.

When we finally moved away, my mother had met my stepfather and started a new life for me, but I had trouble adjusting. My mom thought she could fix me by putting me in a home for kids who needed help. Well, during that six-month stay, not one person asked me why I was angry or what was making me act out. No one even talked about anything. More anger kept building inside of me. I wanted so badly for someone just to talk to me as a person—just sit and talk with me. It never happened.

If one person had asked me, I would have told everything. Instead, I left that home feeling more stupid, dumb, and useless. This was my first chance to tell all and get help, but it didn't help at all.

Years later, I wrote a letter to the board of this home I was sent to and received permission to view my records. When I opened up the file, I was so shocked. I couldn't get past the first page to the next page. The first sentence said that I was given Valium for sedation. I was nine and on Valium. I couldn't read anything else. I got up and left. I didn't want to know anymore. There are times in life when you just can't go back. Your memory blocks things out for a reason. It helps you to survive, and for that I am thankful.

11

Keep people in your life
Who truly love you,
Motivate you,
Encourage you,
Make you happy.

If you know people who do
None of these things
Let them go.
—Author unknown

The first time I ever talked about the abuse was when I was in the sixth grade. I told a friend, and she was so shocked. I told her please, don't tell anyone, and she didn't. What a great friend—but deep down, I so wanted her to tell. I was still carrying this burden.

I hated school in this new town because I have olive skin. I'm Italian, but there was an Indian reservation on the outskirts of town, and everyone thought I was native. I got beat up and picked on. I knew how to throw a good left hook at an early age. I know what being bullied is all about, and I just never fit in at school. I felt like I didn't belong anywhere.

I feel sorry for kids today. I can't imagine with Facebook and texting how I would have handled any of the stuff I went through in school.

If only children could put themselves in the other person's shoes. Every child has feelings, confusion, and pain. We all need to stop and think and not follow the crowd.

It's time to let go of the past

And embrace everything

That awaits you.

—Author unknown

When I was thirteen, my friend and I went to the corner store to get snacks. We went to the fridge at the back of the store, and there was a guy standing there looking at us with his penis hanging out of his shorts. This unexpected sight threw me into a tailspin of despair.

I became angry, violent, and aggressive, and I went crazy for days. I ran away from home. I slept on the beach that night with a friend. Some people brought us blankets, but the police brought me home the next day. I told my mom I was sorry and that I couldn't imagine her worry. I was so full of anger; I couldn't contain my feelings when the police brought us home.

My friend's mom finally said, "What the hell is going on? So a guy flashed you. No big deal!" This is when I finally broke down and blurted out that my father had raped me! The tears came and didn't stop.

It was finally out. My mother now knew. She wanted to get the gun and kill him.

After she calmed down, she asked if I wanted her to call the police. I said no, but I really, really wanted her to. She didn't, and I spent a lot of years angry at her for that. She has said she is sorry for listening to me and not doing that—not doing what a mother should. She said I was so distraught, she was worried that if she called, I would crumble.

I have to remember that she was only twenty-nine at this time. I remember how I felt at that age—I still felt so young. Now I can understand her. We think at that age that we are so mature, but looking back, we were still so young.

We finally went to court over the flasher at the store. Guess what: I got the color of his jacket wrong, so he got off. What a shock!

Well, why say anything here. Another person gets away with it. That's what this child was learning about life.

I tried to get help again at the age of sixteen, telling a counselor about the abuse I suffered as a child.

The first thing out of the counselor's mouth was, "Are you having sex yet?"

I said, "Yes."

His response was, "Don't you feel like a slut?"

Well, I shut down instantly and stopped talking. Ashamed again, and *no* help. Yes, I felt ashamed and like a slut, but wasn't he supposed to help me not feel that way? It was a lost cause.

I tried again in my early twenties. It was a self-help group for incest survivors. The information was great and it was nice to be around people who understood what I went through in my childhood. But instead of an open discussion of the issues we all needed to talk about, it became a man-hater's group. I hated going after a while. I had to have faith that there were good men out there. I needed this faith to survive in this life. I had to leave the group. I didn't want anger in my life. It wasn't good for me.

Inside me, I had faith that the world had to be a good place. I felt it. I wanted to believe it. I wanted to see it. I just knew, deep down. I am so glad I had that gut feeling. It was what kept me going in life.

Some walks you have to

Walk alone.

High School

During my high-school years, my mother and I did not get along. We were both bitter and angry with life. I remember the first time I hit my mother back. I had spilled milk in the kitchen when I was pouring it, and my mom came out of nowhere and smacked me. I saw red. I did not deserve that. I turned around and hit her back. There we were, fistfighting on the kitchen floor, beating the crap out of each other, with my stepdad just feet away watching TV. He didn't do anything, just turned up the volume.

Another time, I called the police on her. She wanted me to shovel two feet of snow in the driveway. I refused to do it; she threw my coat and boots outside and shoved me out the door. Really, aren't there child labor laws against this? Seems kind of funny now that I'm a mom myself.

We had a few fights like this. She was an angry person, and I just hated her back then. After all, she was the one who brought me into this shit. They say we pick our parents. Seriously, why would I pick these two messed-up humans for parents? I know now my soul picked what it needed in order to learn in this journey.

I felt like my mother never protected me when she should have, never cherished and loved me. But I was just a reminder of her mistakes, of her guilt and pain. She hated me because I was a reminder of *him*.

I slept in the back shed one night. I also got kicked out of the house another night and slept under a bridge. There is so much more I could discuss. But we are doing our best to make amends, my mother and I. She is a strong, cutthroat, no-emotion woman, but that's just on the outside. I know she has such tremendous guilt. She thinks she should be tough and I should be more like her. Yes, I'm sensitive, but I like my way. It works for me.

It shows we all deal with life so differently.

As we grow up, we learn that even the one person who
wasn't supposed to ever let us down probably will.
You'll have your heart broken,
and you'll break others' hearts.
You'll fight with your best friend
or maybe even fall in love with them.
And you'll cry because time is flying by.
So take too many pictures, laugh too much,
forgive freely, and love like you've never been hurt.

Life comes with no guarantees,
No time-outs, no second chances.
You just have to live life to the fullest.
Tell someone what they mean to you.
Tell someone off, speak up,
Dance in the pouring rain,
Hold someone's hand,
Comfort a friend.
Fall asleep watching the sun come up, stay up late,
Be a flirt, and smile until your face hurts.
Don't be afraid to take chances
Or fall in love, and most of all live in the moment.
Because every second you spend angry or upset
Is a second of happiness you can never get back.
—Author unknown

We came home one evening from my aunt's funeral to find out someone had broken into our house. They stole a lot of things like jewelry, clothes . . . and my underwear. How embarrassing is it when a police officer brings you your dirty underwear to identify? Seriously! I can laugh as I write this now, but I did not laugh at the time.

They kept stealing things off our clothesline, and we had a big willow tree in the backyard that someone would sit in and watch us. It got to the point where we had to have a police officer living at our house to protect us and try to catch the person. After a few months of this, we had a huge takedown in our backyard. Five police cars and numerous officers everywhere were chasing this man. Finally he was caught. He was charged on sixteen counts and left town shortly after.

I kind of have to laugh at this part as I write my story. Again, this was all I knew. What was normal? I really had no idea. This is *my* normal.

During these years, I still tried to know my father. I felt as if the abuse had never happened. I really thought he was a great guy; I wanted *that* side of him. Although the memories and thoughts never, I mean *never*, go away—they're in your head every day, always—I wanted that dad, someone to love me.

My mother actually sent me to live with him at one point. I said okay, but I was still angry that she sent me away. There was no abuse at that time, but of course, it was still in my head. I was going back to the town where it all happened. I just wanted my dad, and I wanted to believe so badly that it never happened.

To this day, every time I drive into that town, I feel my stomach tie up in knots.

Nothing we do ever goes away
Until it has taught us
What we need to know.
—Pema Chödrön

I was still in high school when I met the boy who would become the father of my children. It was not a healthy relationship, but again, that's what was normal for me. I moved in with my aunt and uncle two hours away for a while to get some distance from him, but that only made us want each other more. Who knew? Silly me. Back home I came. We had to be together! We fell back into the same routine. Nothing had changed.

After we finished writing our grade-twelve exams, we went back-roading. It was the thing to do back then: get a group together, load up the car with booze, and drive down the back roads. Funny thing is, though, I didn't drink back then. But I sure did go along for the ride.

As we headed out of town for our booze cruise, it started to rain. We were going fast; the driver of the van lost control, and we flew through the air and went end over end a few times.

It was a bad scene. I remember getting out of the van and falling to the ground. First there was a light drizzle of rain on my face, and then, after a while, it was like boulders, like Chinese water torture. We had to wait an hour for an ambulance. We were on a back road, and the driver had to run a couple of miles to find a house to call from. There were no cell phones back then.

There were seven of us, and thank God, we all lived. One girl went through the windshield and landed beside the van. We didn't wear seatbelts back then.

The van was destroyed. We were rushed to the hospital. I had to have knee surgery and received thirty-seven stitches across my back. I had ripped my back open. If it had been one millimeter more, I would have been paralyzed. I know I had a guardian angel watching over me that evening. There's no way we all walked away from that without angels protecting us.

Because of that accident, I didn't drive until I was twenty-six years old. I just couldn't get behind the wheel. My fear from the accident would overcome me and destroy me to the point that I was not able to bring myself to drive.

My boyfriend had no such fear. After the accident, he thought it was hilarious to speed down a winding road with the lights off on the truck. He enjoyed this kind of humor. Needless to say, it only added to my fear of driving. I'd freak out, cry, and scream for him to let me out of the car. And so he did—on a back road in the country, all alone at midnight. Thank goodness I knew the people who came by half an hour later to take me home.

And yes, I still kept dating him. I *married* him. Remember, this is all I knew.

I have no regrets about this relationship. I have two of the most amazing children, and for that I am grateful. We have talked, and we are great friends now. We were young, stupid, and insecure—but I know he would be there for me, and I would be there for him.

The 3 Cs of Life

Choices, chances, changes

You must make a choice

To take a chance

Or your life will never change.

—Author unknown

My Children

I was twenty-one years old when I had my daughter, and I was so happy. Finally, I had someone in my life who would love me, someone I could devote all my love to. I needed her in this world.

And yes, I had my daughter on purpose. Yes, I was one of those girls, one who came from a sad life and just wanted to give love and be loved. Don't shake your head at every young girl who has a baby, for you don't know her journey.

I had been pregnant once before, at eighteen, but I had an abortion. I so wanted that baby, but everyone said *don't*. All I wanted was just one person to say, "Do it," and I would have, but no one did. So sadly, I didn't.

To that heavenly soul, I am so sorry, my love.

When I was eight months pregnant with my daughter, my half sister—my birthfather's daughter—passed away. My beautiful sister was born September 24. She also died in September, and my birthday is in September. It's always a sad reminder of that time.

She was diagnosed with a brain tumor, and one year later, she passed away to be an angel. The day of her funeral, my father leaned over and said to me, "I am so sorry for what I've done. This is God's punishment."

Did I just hear that? Yes, yes I did! I needed to hear that, and I needed to know it did really happen and I wasn't crazy. I was lucky that way. So many victims of this crime are told it's not true, it didn't happen. I just can't imagine that.

I believe my sister was also abused, as her mother talked to my mom at one time to discuss something that happened. I remember her sitting at the kitchen table, although my mother will deny this.

During the funeral, it was made clear that I was not a part of this family. During the service, not once was it mentioned that the deceased had a sister, not even in the obituary in the paper. That hurt. I knew I didn't belong in any family, but wow, that did hurt. I now felt more worthless than I had felt before. I was so hurt that they hadn't called me when they knew she was near the end of her life. I felt so guilty that I wasn't there.

Years later, I went to an amazing medium in Alliston. My sister came through—this was her first time to come through to me. She said she knew what happened at the funeral, and she assured me I'm family to her. I know today she is my protection. I feel closer to her now than ever before. I think of her every single day.

When I was twenty-three years old and pregnant with my son. I went to my father's for a visit, as I was living in the area. Yes, I was still trying to know my father. Trying to bury the past. I made sure my children were never ever left alone with him at any given moment. His actions were disgusting, but I was still trying to have my children know the good in their grandfather.

After my sister's death, my father and stepmother applied to be part of a group that pairs children with adults. For some insane reason, they were granted permission to proceed with helping a boy and his little sister. I thought, *This can't be happening . . .* but maybe this is what they needed and all would be okay. I try to see the good in everyone. My friends say this is my downfall.

I went over to visit, and my stepmother was playing a game with the brother. I did not know where the little sister was. I wanted to throw up. My gut was screaming at me, *Where's the little girl?* I was told that she was downstairs in the computer room. I turn around and went to the basement door, which was now shut. I opened the door and looked down to see that the computer-room door was also shut. I wanted to throw up. I felt it, I knew it, something was so wrong. I just stood there. I couldn't move or talk. I didn't know what to do. I wanted to scream and shout, but I froze. I was that little girl in an instant, all over again. I couldn't do anything. I turned and left the house.

Soon after, they were no longer involved with the organization. They said it just wasn't for them. To this day, I wonder. I feel so guilty for that little girl. I am so sorry I didn't help you. So sorry!

Daisy Ann Rhodes

This is your life.
Take responsibility
For your actions.

So now, at this time, I was pregnant with my son. I just knew it was a boy. I knew it. The ultrasound said it was a girl, but I kept saying no, it's a boy. I felt it. And I was depressed and angry about it. I was bringing a child who would become a man into this world. I hate to admit it, but I was scared to death. How could I do this?

The second he was born, I was so happy. I fell in love instantly. I vowed to raise this child to be a good man.

Raising him was a joy. He was always kind, and he loved his mom. Truly, he was *normal*. Having him was healing. I knew he was going to be a good young man.

After having him, I had my tubes tied at twenty-three years old. I was surprised that a doctor would do it, but I am so glad. I had what I needed in life: two beautiful children.

My daughter is a lot like her father—the dry sense of humor, the enjoyment of taunting people. She's a redheaded Scorpio, need I say more? She was a strong-willed child to raise and saucy, oh yes, yes she was. I hear now this would be considered child abuse, but I put hot sauce on her lips if she was rude. She laughed at soap. She hated the hot sauce, but she always had to have the last word, and the last word is something that belonged to me. So battle we did.

Nevertheless, my daughter is one of the funniest ladies I know. She makes me belly laugh. I knew her strong will and independence would benefit her in later life. I admire her and who she is. I am honored that she is my daughter. It is because of her I got the travel bug and have traveled all over. She showed me the strength she had, which in turn gave me the strength to live outside of my comfort zone.

My son is more like me, sensitive and caring. I noticed at a young age that he liked his money, and I knew he would be able to look after himself. He had a lot of health issues in the early years, though. He was born tongue-tied and didn't really talk until he was six years old. He had to go through a lot of surgeries—nose, tonsils, sinus, and ears. Though I didn't play favorites with my children, he did need more attention, which did not sit well with his sister. She lost out on some *me* time, and I still feel guilty for that.

From when he was a preteen, my son was learning how to lay tile. He always knew he wanted to run his own business some day. Both my kids are hard workers. Both know how to save money. My daughter saved hers to buy a horse, my son to buy a dirt bike, snowmobile, jet ski, riding lawnmower, and a car at the age of sixteen. I wanted to teach them that you have to work hard for what you want. No one will get it for you. I'm very proud—no, *honored*—that they are independent, amazing adults.

I did my best as a mother. Was I perfect? God, *no*. I made a lot of mistakes, but I know I must have done something right. I let them be themselves. I worked hard. I had nothing for myself. We were poor, and they didn't know it. I was told that I could move to government housing, but I refused. I put them in a nice townhouse. I could not afford it, but I wanted them to never know that kind of life.

They were always dressed nice. I wore used clothes from my sister. They got to try all the sports they wanted to try, and play with all the new toys that came out. I wanted them to have a childhood! I wanted them to have what I never had. It was worth the struggle and every hardship that I went through—worth it all.

Raising these children has been my greatest achievement in life, and I am so proud of who they have turned out to be and how they live their lives. They are my dream come true. I was sent amazing angels. Thank you, God!

Years ago, a young girl was raped and murdered in an Ontario town in which my father was living at the time. I always wondered if he did it. They had some suspects and someone was wrongly convicted. Years later, when that person was let off, I was asked to give DNA to rule my father out as a suspect. I had to, for the first time, go into details about the abuse I suffered. Nothing is more intimidating and embarrassing, nothing makes you feel more vulnerable, than doing that. Just imagine what it's like for an innocent child to have to do that, if I had issues about it even at my age. My father was cleared of the crime, but what a thing to have to go through. It was a relief . . . but then again, it wasn't.

One day, while hanging out with my niece, it just hit me. I had one of those moments I never had raising my own kids. I don't think, emotionally, I would have been able to handle it. I turned and said to my sister, "She's so innocent. How could anyone ever do such a thing?" For the first time, I really saw what innocence looks like. She was so happy and carefree. It just hit me. I remember so vividly just sitting there shaking my head. I was so happy my children and my niece never had to endure the things I did.

When I finally had enough strength to walk away from my efforts to have the father I just couldn't have, I had to tell my children their grandpa would no longer be in their lives. They asked why, and I replied, "I'll tell you if you want to know, but you may be hurt by what I tell you."

They wanted to know, so I told them he molested me. They just said okay. They didn't want to know more, but they understood and agreed with me that they were better off without him.

Relationships

As you can surely guess, I'm not good at relationships. I take a lot of crap because I want to fix them, but I can also turn off my feelings and move on pretty quickly. As most abuse victims would agree, we have the ability to shut our feelings off so that we can get through things. People ask how I can shut off so quickly. It's called *survival*.

Have I always been faithful? *No!* I am not innocent by any means, but it's because I have to be able to shut down and shut off. Any survivor will understand what I mean. All I know is anger from my mom and betrayal from my father. I wonder, *Can I handle normal?* I'm used to confusion. I find normal boring, yet I think I want it. I've been learning so much about myself this past year, and as I write this, my story, I can see how confused I've been.

I spent nine years with the father of my children, only one of them married. We were young, and mistakes were made. I'm sure there were bets at the wedding as to how long we would last. Bless all our friends and their phony smiles. The reception was a blast.

My mother pulled over a block from the church and begged me not to get married. But I had to, for the children. I had to try to make us a family. It only took to our honeymoon before we were both yelling, "I want a divorce!"

After our son was born, our relationship deteriorated. Let's just say the police were called a lot. He had such a dry sense of humor. We were both stubborn. Once he held me down, and I couldn't get up until I ate all my pizza crust. He found this humorous, not abusive.

There were two years in a row when he walked away from the children for the summer. He would always pick a fight right before the May long weekend. On that Friday, he would not show up for the children at day care. I would get a phone call from the day care around seven saying that the children were still there. It wasn't until October that he would come back around.

When we got a repeat the following year, I was able to see the pattern. He wanted to do his own thing in the summer. Again he picked a fight on the Friday of the long weekend. The children this time were at the door sitting on their suitcases, waiting for their dad to pick them up. They kept saying, "Dad will come." Finally, at ten, I put them to bed heartbroken. It killed me. You can hurt me but *not* my children.

I let the summer go, but when October came, I was down and ready for action. Late at night, around two, I went to his house and waited for him to come home so I could confront him. I told him either he sees the children and never lets them wait for him again, or he goes off and does his own thing and never sees the children again.

I yelled at him, "This is it! Grow up! Don't you ever hurt my children again!"

I'm happy to say that things changed after that day. He never stood the children up again. He was the dad they needed every day, not just when it was convenient for him. He traveled all over with them. He was the one who took the children for a vacation out west. That's when my daughter got the "bug" for the west.

She would move out there later in life. She always called it home. I think her soul had been there before

We had our moments, my ex-husband and I. We both looked after the children differently, but he loved them and that's all I wanted—for them to have a father.

My second relationship ended after eight and a half years. It took me, honestly, three years to get over this one. We were good together but drifted apart. I am so happy for him now. He is with the girl he was meant to be with, and he has a beautiful family. To this day, he is an amazing friend to my son and an amazing mentor. How grateful I am for that.

This is the man who tried to teach me how to drive a car with a standard transmission. I ended up through a fence, four feet from the water, and I almost landed on a $100,000 yacht. Needless to say, I drive an automatic.

I remember so vividly the year our relationship fell apart. He was drinking and out with the boys a lot, while I was home with my children. Funny, now I am so much like he was then— carefree and fun.

He started going out and not coming home. He started going through this anger stage. He hated his job—he wanted to run his own business, but I wanted the safe secure job for him and for our family. He also wanted children, and I couldn't have any. I should have followed my instincts. I knew this would bring up issues. I remember at the start of our relationship asking if he would be okay without children of his own. He said yes, but my gut was telling me otherwise. We really should listen to our gut. But we choose to ignore it, as I did with him.

We tried counseling, but we were both already going in different directions. I remember our very last weekend together, when he didn't come home from the night before. I just knew it was over. I lay in bed in my PJs and cried all day long. I knew this was it. It was over.

When we ended, I wanted to end my life. It took everything I had not to drive into a Mack truck. I had to go on antidepressants. I'm so glad my angels were watching over me. I was searching, asking God, *Please tell me why I am here, why?* I didn't get it. He was a good man. We were just two different people at that time.

After this split, it was less than two weeks before I met someone else. I was so hurt, I would have grabbed on to anyone. It's like these men can spot us a mile away. Weak and vulnerable. I met someone with a very strong, aggressive personality. This guy was a controlling, jealous man. The funny happy girl become quiet and didn't talk.

His coworkers saw the change in me. They saw the signs and knew something was up, and they let their sergeant know he needed to be talked to. I was called into the station for questioning. I wouldn't say he was abusive, I just told them he needed help with his anger. Again, I just wanted him to get help.

My family turned the tables on me, trying some reverse psychology. Instead of expressing their concern while I defended him, they told me what a great guy he was and assured me we would work through it. Guess what the effects were? Amazing. I was shocked and started to see how upsetting he was.

One night, after I'd just had an emergency hysterectomy, he became outraged that I hadn't done the dishes. He grabbed me off the couch and started shoving me around and yelling at me. My twelve-year-old got out of bed and started yelling that this man had no respect for anyone. In that instant, it was over. After we split, I realized what my family had done with changing their reactions. Good job!

When was I going to get this? *Stop trying to fix everyone else and look at yourself.* There was someplace inside of me that I was so afraid to go. I did not want to feel that pain.

I had met a young man I wanted nothing from other than a kiss, but it always went further. I would say no, but he didn't listen and wouldn't stop. You instantly go into that survival mode and shut down, just to get it over with. I think this is what's called *date rape*. I can't imagine how many people have said no and were ignored.

Everyone makes mistakes in life,
But that doesn't mean they
Have to pay for them
The rest of their lives.

Sometimes good people make *bad* choices.
It doesn't mean they're bad;
It means they're humorous.
—Author unknown

My next relationship lasted one year. This was a very peaceful and calm relationship. We were more like best friends. I healed so much that year. He had property on the water, and I went down almost every day and just sat by the water. It was so calm. I was able to be me. Water is my soul. It's the one place that brings me peace and calm.

It was when he mentioned marriage that I instantly backed off. I had to go. I hurt this amazing man, but my leaving was a blessing in disguise for him.

The money he had saved up for the ring, he decided to use to go have laser work on his eyes. When they do this, they do blood work to make sure you're healthy. They found out he had leukemia. It never would have been detected if this had not happened. I am so glad he is here today and happily married to the one he was really meant to be with. I will always cherish the time we had together, and I know that everything happens for a reason. This relationship taught me that.

In life you'll realize

There is a purpose for everyone you meet.

Some will test you,

Some will use you,

And some will teach you.

But most importantly

Some will bring out the best in you.

—Author unknown

And then, I met a man who changed my family's life, and who I ended up hurting dearly.

Everything happened so fast. We met at the end of April, bought a house in July, got engaged in August, moved all our children into the new house in September, and got married the following April. We had an instant family and four teenagers—fifteen, sixteen, seventeen, and eighteen years of age—in one house. Might I add three of them were teenage girls with all different personalities?

We had a few growing pains, but we made it work. We had the most amazing family. We got all the kids through high school, college, and university. We had family dinners, and we all would stay at the table for an extra hour just to talk. All in fun, we would bribe my son to do things for money—like snort Tabasco sauce for ten dollars. He did that, so we offered another ten dollars to snort Wasabi. He did it, and the next day he had to go to the hospital for an eye and sinus infection. But man, we laughed so hard.

Another time, my son agreed to jump into Georgian Bay on Easter weekend for twenty dollars. It was freezing that day, but he did it, and he didn't think it was so bad. He figured that for ten dollars more, he'd do it again. Well, the next time was hilarious. We had to help him out, and he couldn't even walk to the car.

The girls borrowed corn from the neighbors' cornfield to eat, only to find out it was cattle corn. We had so many laughs and a few fights, but we were a family!

One Christmas, we had no snow, so we got all the kids together, hooked up the trailer, went down to the arena, and started to shovel snow into the trailer. We put it all over the front yard so we would have snow on Christmas morning. The neighbors had a great laugh.

When the kids were out of school, we decided to move to the town closest to my husband's work. This is where life changed for us.

I was so excited I was going to be close to the beach. Water is my soul; it calms me and gives me such peace. It just felt so right for me, and I was so ready to leave the job I'd had had for almost ten years. There was a lot of tension at work. They had hired a new manager who was making advances on the young teenage girls who worked there. We had put a report in to human resources, and guess what? The head office said he was innocent, so the managers and most of the staff decided that if this was how we were protected, this was not a company we wanted to work for.

So everything about the move was falling into place. The move changed me. I had never felt so free and calm, so alive. I was meant to be there. It felt so right for me—but everything changed in our marriage at this exact time.

With no children around, my husband started treating me as if I were a child. At the same time, he wanted to age me, telling me to let my hair go gray, to wear older clothes. I am not that kind of lady. I didn't like him trying to change me. This is when I started to rebel and shut down.

I have always been lucky to look younger than I am, but he looked his age with some gray. People were starting to make comments, and they would think I was out with my dad. They'd say, "Oh, you're out for a hike with your dad today!"

I would laugh, of course. It didn't sit well with him, though, and it really didn't sit well with me either. I was having a hard time being intimate with him because people were saying these things. It was hard on me and on him. He knew my past, and in the bedroom he treated me like a victim. He saw me that way, and that is not what I wanted. I wanted him to see me as the sex kitten I thought I was—*Fifty Shades of Grey*, bring it on—but it was not meant to be.

I also wanted to start my own business, and he said it wouldn't work. I felt so discouraged and not supported. I tried so hard to tell him what I needed. He wouldn't budge or listen. We tried counseling, but it was too late.

Did I step out on him at this time? Yes, I did. I'm not proud of it. I hurt him deeply, and I lost an amazing family. It was the wrong way to deal with our problems.

It was finished within weeks. The guilt was there, but again, I was able to shut off instantly.

When I left, I did start my business, and it is doing very well. I am happy and less stressed and very proud of myself.

It was after I left that he said he should have listened. But we all do that, don't we? We have talked and know we both failed, but we are friends, and he's still to this day there when I need him. But I lost the closeness with his daughters, especially the oldest. I deserve that, and I am living sadly with that. I do take full ownership of my actions. But trust me, meeting the man I did next, I got my karma back. I was about to learn a hard lesson.

In my life
I've lived, I've loved,
I've lost, I've missed,
I've hurt, I've trusted,
I've made mistakes,
But most of all
I've learned.
—Author unknown

When I cheated, I met a man who would take me down the hardest road of my life and test me in every way possible. I hit the bottom hard, and I fell into a million pieces.

I met this guy and the first night I met him, I wanted nothing to do with him. I even told my girlfriend, "Keep that guy away from me, he won't leave me alone."

We laughed about him bugging me. He was not anything like who I would think about being with, and I was still married. That wasn't even on my mind.

The next day, he contacted me again. I said, "We are only going to be friends," but he kept contacting me over and over, texting. He was a very persistent guy.

I now know this is his personality—that controlling part of him—but damn, you just don't see it until after. He was determined and was not going to take no for an answer. His persistence intrigued me. I finally said, "Fine. We will go to the beach." I don't know what happened, but that's all it took. His aggressiveness I liked; I wanted more. I was instantly hooked. His strong will and power took control over me.

I was heading for disaster. He was also married, I soon found out. He wasn't too well-liked by many—by anyone, really—but that also intrigued me.

He said his marriage was over; he never went home and she never came up. He was a contractor working away from home, so I listened to everything he said about this sad pathetic marriage he was in. Now I know he was doing the same thing at home. He put you on such a huge pedestal—how could you not believe him?

He was so controlling and jealous. One time I was talking to one of his friends at his house. I didn't think anything of it, but oh, he did. Later that night when we went to bed and were being intimate, he was very aggressive. He slapped my ass so hard, I had a welt of a handprint on my butt for two weeks. He said that was my punishment for talking to his friend. "Don't do it again."

I was so shocked and hurt that I couldn't even get angry.

The next day, he put me back up on my pedestal. He loved and adored me. I had never had this before. It did feel amazing to be loved this way.

Things slowly changed. It's so slow you don't even realize it. At first he loved the way I dressed, but slowly he didn't want me wearing certain things. No one should see if I have breasts. They only belonged to him.

I would go out, but after so long he kept texting and calling me to come home, and I knew he was getting mad. It was easier to come back to his place than deal with all that, and when I got there he loved and admired me.

He bought a lot of things for me. I know it was to buy me, to buy my love. Another way of controlling me, which I see now.

When we would fight, he would have very aggressive sex, and a couple of times I said, "No, this is not going to happen today, I don't want to."

He said, "You're mine, you don't say no to me." Again, is this rape? It felt wrong to me, but he was right. I was his. He suckered me in each time with, "No one knows me like you. You are the only one who can calm me down." I felt I loved this man and couldn't live without him. I wanted to and I tried, but his persistence kept me in the relationship.

I tried so hard to fix him, to heal him. I helped him deal with his father's death, and he took me to the grave. He was trying to be the man he wanted to be; he knew he had anger issues and wanted my help. He couldn't do it without me. I so believed in him.

But throughout the whole relationship, he was cheating. People tried to tell me, but he was always so convincing, and I thought, *No way, he wouldn't cheat on me.* I was on such a pedestal. *No way!*

Remember, I started out as his mistress. Everyone hates the mistress. We don't go looking for this to happen, and once we realize what we have gotten ourselves into, it's just too late to turn back. It's true—the other woman does not walk away with her Prince Charming. You think that you are special, but if he can have a mistress and a wife, he will do it to you or is doing it already.

He and his wife did finally split up, but the mistress never is *the one*. There are so many stories I could share, but I think you get how it was. When he tells you that you are crazy, it's because he is guilty. Trust me, so many "other women" tried to tell me it would never work and said everything I'm saying now. So to anyone in this situation, you deserve better. Never be that woman. You are better than that, and you deserve true love.

Our relationship was always in turmoil, but for me, I could handle it. I handled turmoil well. I lost friends left and right, though. And I was losing myself.

We started to part ways, but it was easier said than done. I got away for six months, but he could always get me back. I would try it again for a day or a week or two, but it was always the same. At this point, we both just couldn't end it. His friends finally came to me to tell me he had been cheating since the beginning, almost twenty girls. I was devastated.

I went back for another week. He played on how he couldn't live without me. I asked if he had cheated. He got so mad he dragged me across the garage by my hair and asked, "How dare you not trust me!"

Finally, there were so many lies that he couldn't keep them straight. He went away for a weekend and said he was at his mom's, that she had taken him to get anger management for the weekend. The guys he worked with sat me down. They liked me, and they wanted me to understand that he went to see a girl for the weekend. I searched his house and found his suitcase under a tarp with his camera and pictures. Let's just say I saw red, and I pulled a Carrie Underwood song on him.

I got home afterward and I was emotionally crushed. I wanted to kill myself. I begged God to kill me. I'd had enough. I couldn't do this anymore. I knew if I stayed alone any longer, I was going to overdose. This wasn't for me. I reached out to a friend and said, "Please take me to the hospital or I'm going to kill myself."

Do you have any idea how embarrassing it is to have a security guard sit outside your door at the hospital? I put my big-girl britches on and after crying for two days straight, I knew I had to get myself together. My family reminded me how my niece loved me and needed me. For her, I could do this, but I was searching, asked God, *Why, why, why?*

He still tried to contact me after this. He had gotten mad at me for telling someone what happened and said, "Don't talk to anyone again or I will kill you."

That was it, No more. I told the police, "This has to stop." I finally wanted off this roller-coaster ride.

Be soft.

Do not let the world make you hard.

Do not let pain make you hate.

Do not let the bitterness steal your sweetness.

Take pride that even though

The rest of the world may disagree,

You still believe it to be

A beautiful place.

—Kurt Vonnegut

Finding Purpose

My last relationship really was the hardest journey of my life. But the end result was, I got all the answers about my life and why this has been my journey.

I know now why I am here, why I've gone through my lessons, and what my life's purpose is. It's to take my wisdom and pain and use them to help others.

I owe all that to Louise Hay and her book *You Can Heal Your Life*. This book and attending her "I Can Do It" seminar have changed my life. I will be forever grateful.

I'm stronger because I had to be.
I'm smarter because of my mistakes.
I'm happier because I have to
Overcome the sadness I've known,
And I'm wiser because I have
Learned from life.
—Author unknown

If you're in a relationship and he slowly starts to change you, how you dress, be yourself. Don't change—it's who you are. If it's true love, he will want you to be you.

If he starts keeping you from your friends or doesn't like any of your friends, pay attention to all of the signs. Stop and see how the patterns are all the same. When your friends and family come to you, stop and listen. They love you. That feeling you get, follow it. We all really need to do this.

I tried counseling, but again, it didn't work for me. I tried again, and she just sat there repeating the same stuff. I knew I had to take things into my own hands and heal myself. I wanted this; I was ready. I asked the counselor so many times to help me deal with my father, but she would only talk about the present. You can't deal with the present without dealing with the past.

I grabbed the book *The Secret* to read. It helped. I was on the right path. The right books kept coming to me. I was finally listening to the universe, letting it guide me to where I needed to be. Books were falling into my lap.

Then I read *You Can Heal Your Life* by Louise Hay. This was my bible. My whole life changed. I felt that I was on a calmer level, and I was. The answers were being given to me. I was meeting people who thought like these books, and things just fell into place.

While attending the "I Can Do It" conference, at one point I just started crying. I let go of so much that weekend.

I left knowing my journey was for a reason, and I left knowing the path that was ahead of me.

I also attended a oneness group that gave blessings, and *wow*, the healing I was getting from going to the meetings. I was healing, and inside, I now knew that I had the capability of helping others.

I have met so many people who have sent me messages about how much my positive comments have meant to them. Knowing

I've gone through tough times has helped them—knowing they can come out on top. They felt like I was talking to them and I was there when they needed it most. I was helping others, and I didn't even know it. That's all I wanted, to let others know they are not alone. Someone does understand. So many people have secrets they need to let out, talk about, and deal with.

I can see both sides of things now. I see and understand so much. I feel people's energies. I feel their pain. I can tell when their energy is low. Everything happens to teach our soul.

I now let the universe take me where I need to go. I live so simply now. I gave most of my belongings to my amazing son, who at twenty-two bought a house so he could start his life. I have given away things to others who have needed it. I don't need material possessions.

I live for today. You can't worry about tomorrow. I live each moment now and try to see the good in everything, in every moment.

I get stressed. I reach out to someone to see the positive, and I take deep breaths to center myself again. Taking three deep breaths really works. Just try it. Take three deep breaths right now and relax. You just feel so much calmer.

This really is a new era. We need to see that and all live in oneness.

When I meet negative people, I need to remove myself from them. When I have someone close to me. I try to talk with that person, and I gently remind him or her to see the glass as half full. It takes so much stress away when you just take that deep breath.

I can only hope that everyone can become aware. You really do have to learn from each lesson or it will be taught to you over and over again until you can understand.

I am in such a great place to finally be able to feel spirit, and now I understand my body is just the vessel for my soul. This is my soul's journey.

The next time you are somewhere and someone's being rude, instead of getting stressed, just think for a minute. Maybe that person just lost someone, or is worrying about something. How do you know? Maybe that person who just cut you off on the freeway has to hurry home because a child is sick. We get mad constantly. Just be happy and calm. It's contagious!

Just take those three deep breaths and change your attitude.

I wrote my father a letter a couple of years ago just saying, "I forgive you. I will never ever forget, but I forgive you." I needed him to know that I had to let go, to let go for me and my pain, to be at peace, and I am better for it.

He did not respond, but I'm okay with it. Who knows the life he had, why he did the things he did? I know I am a better person for reaching out.

Daisy Ann Rhodes

Someone once asked me

How I hold my head

Up so high after all I've been through.

I said, it's because no matter what,

I am a survivor.

Not a victim.

—Patricia Buckley

I am here to help others. I am no longer angry, just grateful. I wouldn't change my life because it's made me who I am today.

I want to show my love, support, and wisdom to help others. You can go through trauma and still come out on top, positive and grateful for life.

So many of us go down the wrong paths in life. Some go to drugs, alcohol—so many things to try to bury the pain instead of dealing with it. You need to let it go, to live life. Be the amazing person you are meant to be. We are all shining stars! We are special, important, and amazing, every one of us. Don't wait as long as I did to know that you are a special person.

It was after my first relationship with my children's father and during my second relationship that I became bulimic. I was lost in my life and needed control. I couldn't get it anywhere else, but I could have control over what I ate, over my body, over how I looked. This continued for years. It's amazing how people struggle with their body image, how someone can see herself so differently than others do. I would look at myself in the mirror and think that I was heavy.

Finally, one day I was in a friend's wedding, and I saw pictures of myself walking down the aisle. I was shocked at how thin I had become, and I felt my head was too big for my body. I was honestly shocked. At that very moment, my eating disorder came to a halt, and I changed the way I lived.

Now, today, I see why this happened to me. It was the need to have control over myself, over my body. Now I know that I don't have to be thin. It's okay to love your body and your curves, to love the way you were built.

It's amazing how your body can be affected on a long-term basis. I had tooth decay and migraines, and who knows what effect it had on my organs.

If anyone who is reading this is living this way now, please stop and go talk to someone—reach out for help. It is not worth your life. We all need to see our worth, and everyone is different. Everyone has faults; just be yourself. Sometimes we learn the hard way.

Today, I am proud to be healthy, and I have accepted myself the way I was meant to be.

Sometimes people are beautiful.

Not in looks.

Not in what they say.

Just in what they are.

—Markus Zusak

I want all who read this to understand, you are not alone. You are worth your precious life. Each one of us is so unique, so special. If one person doesn't have to go through all I've seen and felt, then I will be blessed.

Please contact me. Please, anyone, if you are feeling alone, just let someone know. This happened to me. I will be there. Counseling isn't for everyone, but please try it first. I know for some, just talking to someone who understands what you've been through is healing. We are all family. My path is to share my journey in life to help others.

God bless my spirits and guardian angels who protect me in this life.

Dear Self:

Please accept yourself more.

Please love yourself.

Please make the right choices.

Please know what is good for you.

And please know that you are not alone.

—Author unknown

When I really started to find myself, I found a sport to bring me to the water. I started to paddleboard. It is the most peaceful and calming activity for me. I started to appreciate the amazing things you can see in the outdoors and nature, the beauty in the world. I found what I needed. If I could get out every day, I would. Find an activity that brings you to your calming place.

I also started a bucket/life list. Yes, my very own list. Everyone should have one—a list of all those things that you really want to do or places you really want to go. The items can be big or small—anything that forces you to get out of your comfort zone and live. Don't just think about it. Go for it!

I was always afraid of heights. I wanted to overcome my fear, so I put getting on the Drop Zone on my bucket/life list. And I did it. I might have gone kicking and screaming, but I did it. It wasn't as bad as I thought, but I did it and that felt amazing. I have traveled to many islands and different beautiful places and have checked a lot off my list. I now live and do what I want instead of sitting back and wishing to do those things in life.

I am so proud of myself for doing this. All I want is for others to know that what and how they feel is normal, and know that they are not alone. I want them to not feel ashamed or embarrassed. We are *not* victims, we are survivors. Hold your head high

For those who have kept these secrets in, let them out, free yourself. Write a letter to your abuser. You don't need to send it, but just let it out. Find someone who will eventually listen, and keep talking.

I have opened myself up to the universe to really see the entire world in all its beauty. I've been to Antigua, Cuba, the Dominican Republic, Panama, Jamaica, and Myrtle Beach. I was lucky enough to have an amazing friend with a boat who took me to the islands of St. Maarten, St. Kitts, and St. Lucia, where I was able to see flying fish, whales, and dolphins in the middle of the ocean with no land on the horizon. I went to Florida and swam with dolphins in their natural environment, as it should be, not caged up.

I did the stingray shuffle and swam with the stingrays. I went to Lake Louise, Myrtle Beach, and British Columbia. The world in all its beauty is right in front of us.

Funny note: During my last relationship, we went to Florida. I was just telling him about karma and how it comes back to you. Out of the blue, a bird pooped all over him. I could not stop laughing, and when I did, all I said was, "See, karma." I still laugh. What perfect timing. Thank you, Father Sky and Mother Earth.

Live for today. Don't keep saying you want do this or that. Do it . . . *live!*

About the Author

I live on the shores of Lake Huron. I have two grown children whom I love and adore. I am an auntie to an amazing little girl. I enjoy paddleboarding, kayaking, days at the beach, and being outside and in my bare feet. Best of all, I love to live to the beat of my own drum.

I am uniquely me.

My Bucket List
My Living Life List

ACTIVITY	TO DO	DONE
Be debt-free		X
Write a book		X
Go to Calgary Stampede	X	
Feed the homeless (I tried to feed them, but they would not take the food)		X
Skinny-dip at midnight		X
Jump in a random pool at midnight	X	
Be the most amazing grandma	X	
Meditate in Thailand	X	
Live somewhere tropical	X	
Climb a mountain by Lake Louise	X	
Exercise every day	X	
Ride my own motorcycle	X	
Visit my ancestors' birthplace in Italy and Holland	X	
Hug a random stranger	X	
Meet Oprah Winfrey	X	
Pray with the Dalai Lama	X	

Take someone to Disneyland	X	
Start a group for children/teenagers who have been abused	X	
Go to a Stanley Cup game	X	
Paddleboard in Hawaii	X	
Visit St. Lucia		X
Go to an NHL playoff game		X
Do the Drop Zone at Wonderland		X
Make peace with my mother		X
Drink wine in the Napa Valley	X	
Forgive my father		X

Now make your own list and start living life today.

I've made mistakes in my life.
I've let people take advantage of me,
And I accepted way less than I deserve.
But I've learned from my bad choices and
Even though there are some things I can never get back
And people who will never be sorry,
I'll know better for next time and
I won't settle for anything less than I deserve.
—Author unknown

Notes

Notes

Notes

Notes

Notes

Notes

Notes

Start Your Letter Today

Dear _____

Innocence Lost

I wrote this book so I can open up to people, so other survivors would not feel alone. Sharing my story was important to me, because I knew if I did it would help someone say, "I felt like that; this happened to me. I want to talk about it." We need to share our stories so we don't all suffer in silence. I hope you feel my feelings and it helps you to learn and understand what others feel. At the end of my story, I want you to say, "I'm going to start living today. My life is worth living."

Manufactured by Amazon.ca
Bolton, ON